discovermore

Economics in Your Community

# Supply and Demand

Sloane Wilden



Britannica®
Educational Publishing
IN ASSOCIATION WITH
THE ROSEN PUBLISHING GROUP

Published in 2024 by The Rosen Publishing Group, Inc.
2544 Clinton Street, Buffalo, NY 14224



Editor: Brianna Propis
Book Design: Rachel Rising

Photo Credits: Cover Gorodenkoff/Shutterstock.com; (series background) Dai Yim/Shutterstock.com; p. 4 GaudiLab/Shutterstock.com; p. 5 Ascannio/Shutterstock.com; p. 6 Hryshchyshen Serhii/Shutterstock.com; p. 7 Drazen Zigic/Shutterstock.com; p. 8 DimaBerlin/Shutterstock.com; p. 9 Nattapol_Sritongcom/Shutterstock.com; p. 11 Tarasyuk Igor/Shutterstock.com; p. 11 S_Photo/Shutterstock.com; p. 12 Ground Picture/Shutterstock.com; p. 13 krithnarong Raknagn/Shutterstock.com; p. 14 stable/Shutterstock.com; p. 15 Matt Benoit/Shutterstock.com; p. 16 Quentin Eastman/Shutterstock.com; p. 17 Me dia/Shutterstock.com; p. 19 Ground Picture/Shutterstock.com; p. 20 Roman Zaiets/Shutterstock.com; p. 21 Kzenon/Shutterstock.com; p. 22 MAGNIFIER/Shutterstock.com; p. 23 Sergey Nivens/Shutterstock.com; p. 25 fizkes/Shutterstock.com; p. 25 A-photographyy/Shutterstock.com; p. 26 RomanR/Shutterstock.com; p. 27 fizkes/Shutterstock.com; p. 28 ViDI Studio/Shutterstock.com; p. 29 Gorodenkoff/Shutterstock.com.

**Library of Congress Cataloging-in-Publication Data**

Names: Wilden, Sloane, author.
Title: Supply and demand / Sloane Wilden.
Description: [Buffalo] : Britannica Educational Publishing, 2024. | Series: Discover more: economics in your community | Includes bibliographical references and index.
Identifiers: LCCN 2023029261 | ISBN 9781641900423 (library binding) | ISBN 9781641900416 (paperback) | ISBN 9781641900430 (ebook)
Subjects: LCSH: Supply and demand--Juvenile literature. | Economics--Juvenile literature.
Classification: LCC HB183 .W55 2024 | DDC 330--dc23/eng/20230707
LC record available at https://lccn.loc.gov/2023029261

Manufactured in the United States of America

# Contents

# Supply and Demand 101

Economics is a social science concerning the production, distribution, and consumption of goods and services. All economies require producers and consumers. Producers make or provide goods and services. Consumers are the people who pay for and use those goods and services.

When a person buys an item at a store or online, they are a consumer—or a person who buys goods and services.

*Jurassic World: Dominion* was the second most popular film of 2022, creating a large demand for toys related to the movie.

The amount of goods consumers want to buy is called demand. The amount companies produce is called supply. The relationship between supply and demand helps set the prices for the goods and services.

If there is a large supply of an item and the demand for the item is low, the price will be low. If there is a small supply and a high demand, the price will be high. For example, suppose there is a new toy that everyone wants, but the producer only made a few. Some consumers might pay a lot of money to make sure they can have one of the few toys. Other consumers will decide to save their money.

## Consider This

How do a producer and consumer work together in the economy? How might one benefit from the other?

# Consuming Goods and Services

Whether or not goods and services are easy to access is determined by supply and demand. A good is an object that people can touch or hold, such as food, clothing, video games, cell phones, and books. Some producers **manufacture** goods, such as clothing and video game systems. Other goods, such as fruits and vegetables, are grown.

Goods are objects you can hold, feel, and touch, and can be found in many places like a store, restaurant, or on the internet.

Services are actions a person does for someone else, such as driving a public or school bus.

A service is an action that a person does for someone else. Bakers, teachers, firefighters, and dance instructors are all people who offer services. Some businesses, such as restaurants, provide both goods and services. The restaurants have food available, as well as people to serve the food.

## WORD WISDOM

**Manufacturing refers to creating something, like goods, by using a machine to mass-produce many of them.**

# Production of Goods and Services

Goods and services are created and provided by producers. They grow things on a farm, make things by hand or in a factory, or provide services. A producer can be an individual person or a company. Many goods are made from natural resources, such as wood, which comes from trees. Wood is used to manufacture pencils, paper, books, furniture, toys, and more. Some goods that are grown, such as cotton, are sold to producers, who use them to make other goods.

Goods, such as jewelry and pottery, can be handmade by someone and sold to others.

Some goods are made from recycled resources, such as the paper in this book.

Producers make goods and services in response to the demand from consumers for a particular item. The more in demand a product is, the more a producer may make to fulfill the demand. The demand will also influence the price of the item. Prices increase if demand for the item increases, making it more **expensive**.

## WORD WISDOM

**Something that is expensive costs a lot of money.**

# Researching

Producers must begin researching a product or service before creating it. This will help them avoid problems. To do that, they have to think about both supply and demand.

Before they make a product or provide a service, they have to know whether there is a demand for the product or the service. The demand is what people want and need. Wants are not the same as needs. Needs are things that people must have in order to survive, or live. Food, shelter, water, and clothing are needs. Video games, cell phones, and trendy sunglasses are wants, which means people would like to have them but do not need them to survive.

**compare and contrast**

Think about the things you need to survive versus the things you'd like to have. Are some more expensive than others? How do needs and wants affect supply and demand?

Water, shelter, and food are needs, because you cannot survive without them.

Do you like ice cream? Of course! However, ice cream is an example of a want, or an item you could live without.

A company has to do research in order to find out if there is a need for a product. If they create a product without knowing if anyone will buy it, they could lose money. After that, the company must think about supply. Supply means how much it can make. It also means how much of the goods and services are already available. If other companies are already making the product, the supply may be very high. In that case, consumers may not pay as much for the product.

Market research is used for a company to learn what new products the public wants, and whether or not they will sell.

It is important for a company to look at how much making a product will cost, such as through knowing the price of raw materials. Wool, fabric, or wood are examples of raw materials.

Companies want to make money, so they need to think about how much consumers will pay for a product. Companies also need to think about how much it will cost them to make a product. That cost includes paying for the raw materials that go into the product, as well as paying the workers who make and sell the product.

## Consider This

If there is a big event planned to take place on a street where a few restaurants are located, how might the owners prepare for more customers that day?

# Raw Materials

In order to make a product, producers must gather raw materials. Raw materials can be things like paper, glue, paint, and string to make a kite, or steel and concrete to make an office building. If there are plenty of materials available, a producer can make many goods. If the materials are rare, or not easy to find, the producer will charge more or is not able to make the item.

A product can be made easily if the materials are easy to find. A kite can be made if a producer has paper, glue, paint, and string easily available.

Some resources are rare, which can make a product more expensive if they are used. One ounce, or 28 grams, of gold is worth more than $1,000.

## Consider This

Natural resources, such as minerals, metals, and plants, are limited. What would happen if we do not carefully use these resources? How could this impact the creation of goods and services?

Raw materials are often referred to as natural resources. A natural resource is something of value people get from the environment, such as air, water, plants, animals, rocks, and minerals. Some resources are renewable, which means they can be replaced or grown back. Trees are a renewable resource. Wood is used to make paper, furniture, houses, toys, and more. New trees can be planted and more can be grown in a short amount of time. Nonrenewable resources cannot be replaced, or they take a very long time to be replaced or grow back. **Fossil fuels** are nonrenewable natural resources. Once they are used, they cannot be replaced.

Trees are a renewable resource because they can be replanted.

Nonrenewable resources, like coal or oil, cannot be easily replaced, making them more expensive. It can take millions of years for them to form.

## WORD WISDOM

**Fossil fuels are made from the decomposed, or rotted, plants and animals that have been locked in Earth's crust for millions of years. Fossil fuels are burned to make heat and energy.**

# Workforce

The production of goods and the services needed to assist the public are made possible through workers. It is the most expensive cost for a producer. A producer must control how many workers it employs and how much it pays them.

When a company sells a product it must take away the cost of the labor and resources that it spent to make the product. Whatever is left is called a **profit**. For example, if a company charges $30.00 for a pair of jeans, it does not make a profit of $30.00. It must pay for the material and the thread that was used to make the jeans. It must also pay for the workers who sewed the jeans. If the jeans cost $5.00 to make, and the cost to buy each pair of jeans is $15.00, then the company's profit is $10.00. It can be difficult for business owners to find the balance between paying workers and making profits.

A person in the workforce is called a laborer. Laborers help make or serve the product. Laborers work in every single type of industry.

## WORD WISDOM

**Profit refers to the amount of money a company receives, which is the amount earned minus the amount spent making the product.**

Imagine this: If a factory that makes jeans has three workers and three sewing machines, the three workers can make 12 pairs of jeans each day. If the owner of the factory hires one more worker, the company can make 16 pairs of jeans. The company can now produce a larger supply of jeans. If it charges the same amount for each pair of jeans, it will make more money by producing 16 pairs.

Factories manufacture many types of goods—from clothing and furniture to toys and electronics.

A worker will be employed in a factory that matches their skills. If they are good at sewing, they might work in a clothing factory.

However, the company has to pay each worker a salary, and it may be more than the extra money the company makes by selling the extra pairs of jeans.

## Consider This

How does a company keep operating if they're making less than they're paying workers? Does this affect the price of the product?

# Global Exchange

Across the globe, businesses buy and sell goods and services between nations. This is called international trade. The citizens of one country may want goods they do not have the resources to make. Under these conditions, countries look elsewhere to find what they need. Some countries sell products to others. These products are called exports. Other countries buy items from other nations. These items are called imports.

A country will import, or bring in, certain goods and export, or send out, others.

International trade helps a process called globalization, which is creating communication and connections between people of different companies and industries worldwide.

International trade affects the supply and demand in both the country that makes the goods and the country that buys the goods. In some cases a product may be made in more than one country. However, one country may be able to make it for less money.

In that case, there may be a greater supply of the product at a lower cost—which increases the product's demand.

## Consider This

Do you think a country makes more money from imports or exports? How do they both help the producers and consumers?

# Two Branches of Economics

Economics is the study of the manufacturing of goods and services and how consumers will pay for those goods and services. There are two main branches of economics. Microeconomics looks at individual consumers and businesses. Macroeconomics is the study of how a whole country's economy works.

People who study microeconomics try to explain why consumers buy one product rather than another. They also look at why companies choose to produce one good or service instead of another. Another area of study is the relationship between workers and their employers.

Microeconomics can explain how a coffee shop sets the prices of its goods and how that will affect the shop's selling of their products.

An economist is someone who studies how and why consumers buy one product over another.

## compare and contrast

Are macroeconomics and microeconomics similar to each other in any way? How are they different?

Many governments use macroeconomics to decide how much tax, or an extra charge on products, to collect.

People who study macroeconomics look at how much all the goods and services that a country produces are worth. They also study economic growth, or how a nation's wealth becomes larger. Economists look at how people create wealth, how they use it, and how different people get different amounts of it.

Governments are interested in macroeconomics as well. A government plays an important role in its country's economy. In some countries, the government decides which goods and services should be produced and sold. It also decides how many goods should be produced and sets the prices for the goods. This is called a planned economy.

The United States of America is considered a free market, but some consider it a mixed market. A mixed market allows the government to **intervene** at times.

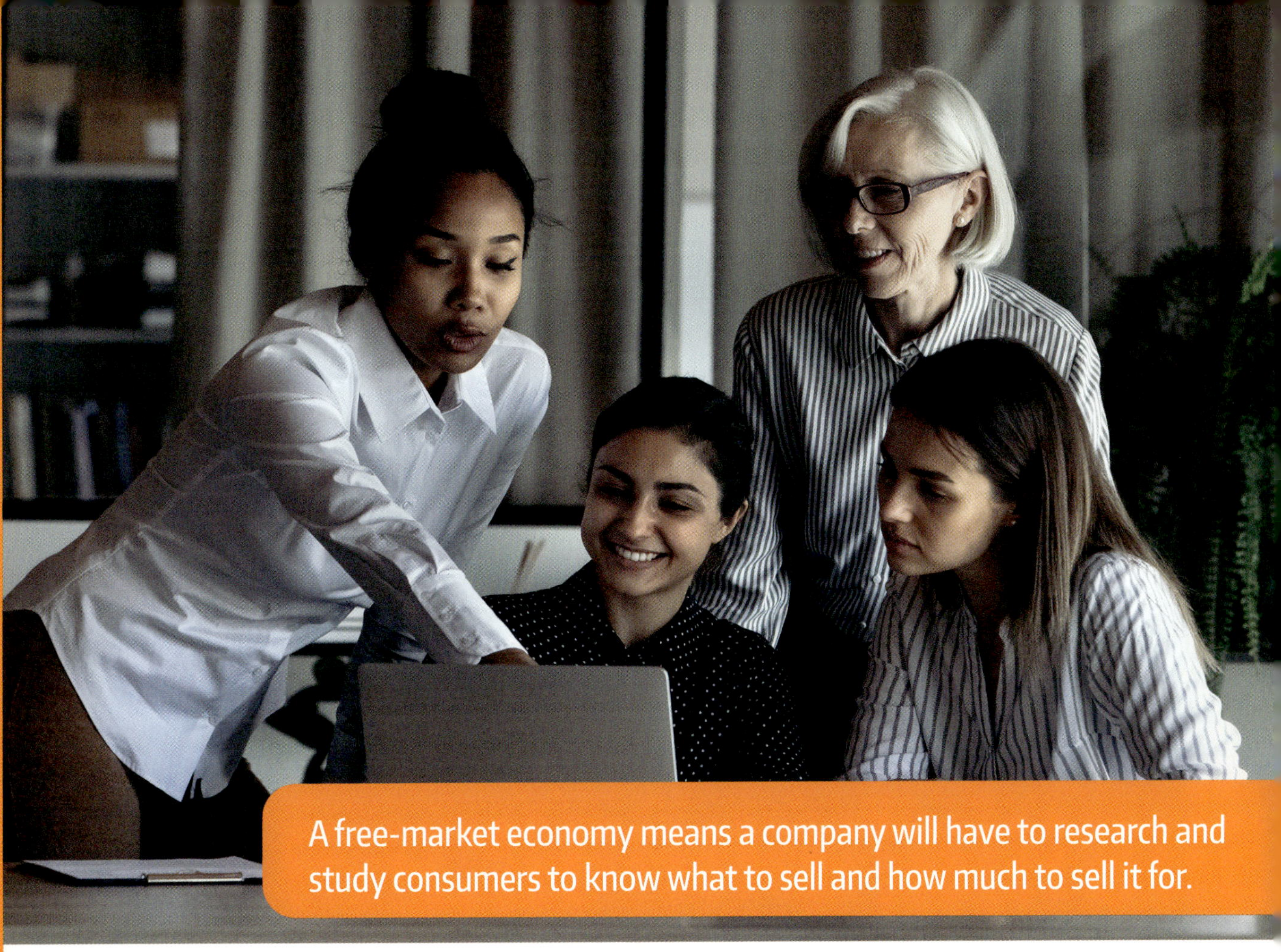

A free-market economy means a company will have to research and study consumers to know what to sell and how much to sell it for.

By contrast, most governments let companies and consumers decide what will be produced—which is called a free market. The government cannot intervene in a free market.

## WORD WISDOM

**To intervene means to tell someone or a company what to do.**

# Unlimited Wants, Limited Needs

Every day, we make decisions about what we need and what we want. You decide what to eat, what to wear, and what games to play. You also decide what you want to buy. You can't have all of the things you want all of the time, so you have to make choices. Yours and everyone else's decisions affect the economy as a whole.

You, as a consumer, play an important part in supply and demand. Each person's wants and needs are important for producers to note in order for the economy to function.

Producers have to make sure they supply enough of a product to meet their customers' demands. If the demand is high, the price will likely increase.

Producers have to make choices as well. They must decide how to use the available resources to make products that people will want to buy. Then, they must try to create enough products that will match the demands of consumers.

## Consider This

If companies do not have enough resources to fulfill a need, how will this affect the production and sale of a product that is made with a limited resource?

# Glossary

**consumer** A person who buys and uses up goods.

**economics** The study of the production and use of goods and services.

**export** A product or service that is created in one country and sent to another country to be sold.

**import** A product or service that is brought into a country from another country.

**international** Involving two or more nations.

**manufacture** To create something out of raw materials.

**market** A meeting together of people to buy and sell.

**production** The act or process of producing or making something.

**profit** The gain or benefit from something. In economics, it is the money that a business keeps after paying costs.

**society** A system or group of living things that depend on each other and usually form a social unit.

**trade** To take part in the exchange, purchase, or sale of goods.

# For More Information

## Books

Flynn, Sarah Wassner. *Not-So-Common Cents: Super Duper Important Facts About Money You Can't Afford to Miss*. Washington, D.C.: National Geographic Kids, 2023.

Kishtainy, Niall. *The Economics Book: Big Ideas Simply Explained*. New York, NY: DK, 2018.

Lee, Kelly. *What Is Supply and Demand? Little Economists*. San Jose, CA: Econ for Kids, 2022.

## Websites

**Economics**
*jr.brainpop.com/socialstudies/economics/*
Learn more about important economics topics, like goods and services and needs and wants, through informative videos and fun games!

**Money and Finance, Supply and Demand**
*www.ducksters.com/money/economics.php*
Money and the economy are explained for you to further learn about.

**Social Studies Economics**
*ny.pbslearningmedia.org/subjects/social-studies/economics/*
Local and global exchange in the economy are made easy to understand with the videos found here.

Publisher's note to educators and parents: Our editors have carefully reviewed these websites to ensure that they are suitable for students. Many websites change frequently, however, and we cannot guarantee that a site's future contents will continue to meet our high standards of quality and educational value. Be advised that students should be closely supervised whenever they access the internet.

# Index